PATTERNS

Ivan Bulloch

Consultants
Wendy and David Clemson

TWO-CAN

2 Looking at Patterns

There are patterns all around us – on brick walls, pavements, on our clothes and on butterflies' wings. A pattern is made when shapes or numbers are put in a sequence and repeated. This book is about exploring patterns.

Look around you. Can you see any patterns? Some patterns are natural, like the patterns of animals' skins and the veins of a leaf. Some patterns are man-made, like the patterns made by a brick wall or the pattern of tiles on a roof. How many different patterns can you spot?

Maths is about patterns and we use pattern to make sense of the world around us. Looking for and making patterns in a wide variety of situations is essential to children's aesthetic and intellectual development.

4 Spirals

Make a patterned snake to hang from
the ceiling.

Painting a Spiral

● Draw a spiral on a
piece of card. Start from
the edge of the card and
gradually spiral in
towards the centre. You
may need to draw a few
spirals for practice first.

● Cut the snake out, starting
from the end of the spiral on
the edge of the card.

● Paint a snake pattern on your spiral. Diamonds or triangles look good.

● Ask a grown-up to thread a piece of cotton through the middle of the spiral. Make a knot in the end of the thread. Now you can hang your snake up.

● You could decorate your snake with coloured paper shapes instead of painting it.

Spirals occur in nature and children can investigate them mathematically when they are older.

6 Beads

Threading beads is a good way to make a pattern. Look around your home or school for things to use as beads. Here are some ideas for making your own beads.

Paper Beads
● Clue together two pieces of coloured paper. Tear out a triangle shape. Roll the shape around a pencil and stick down the narrow end.

● Make a simple paper bead with a long strip of coloured paper. Roll it around a pencil, then stick down the end. You could decorate the paper before making your beads.

Pasta Beads
● Pick pasta shapes with holes through the middle.
● Paint the pasta with poster paints and leave to dry.

Clay Beads

● We used the type of clay which hardens by itself to make these beads.
● Make a small ball of clay and ask a grown-up to make a hole in it with a knitting needle or a cocktail stick.

Sorting Beads

How many types of beads have you made? How many types of beads have you found?
● Try sorting your beads into different colours or different shapes.
● Look at the next page for ideas on threading beads.

Gives practice in categorising and sorting.

Beads to Find!

If you look hard, you should be able to find lots of things to use as beads. We used straws, plastic beads and even peanuts. Can you think of anything else you could use?

Now you can try making some patterns with your beads.

● Use string or shoe-laces to thread the beads into a necklace.
● Pick two sorts of beads. Thread one sort, then another on to the string.
● Look at the patterns on this page. Can you make up your own bead patterns?

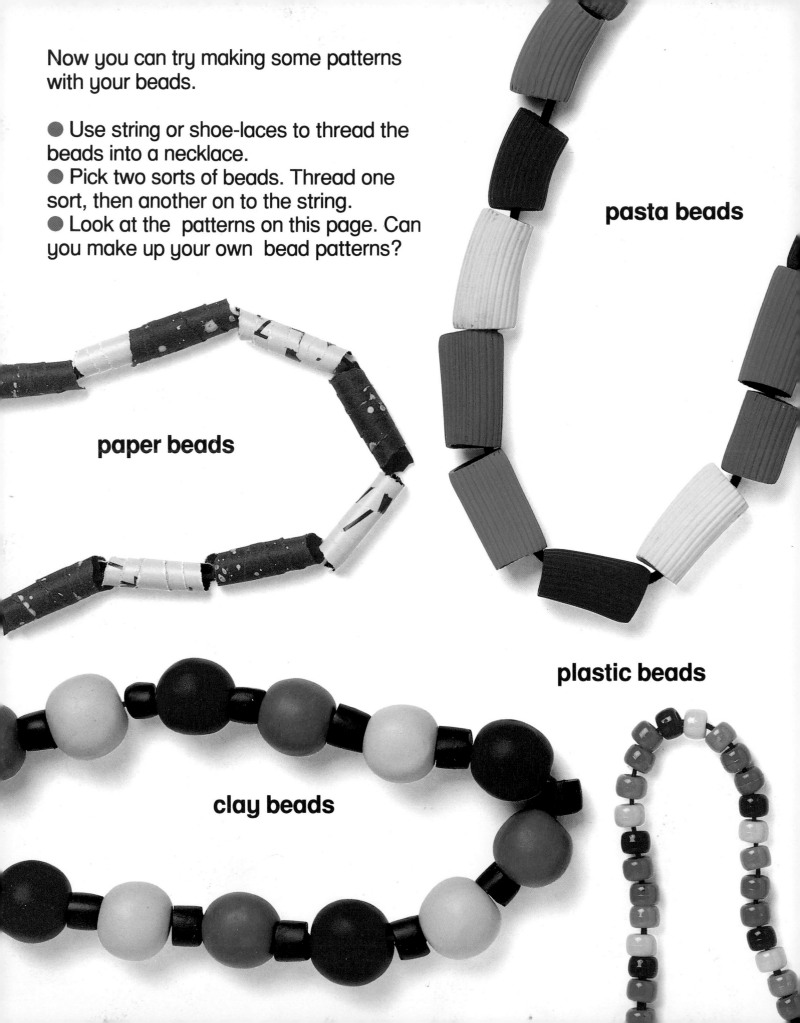

pasta beads

paper beads

plastic beads

clay beads

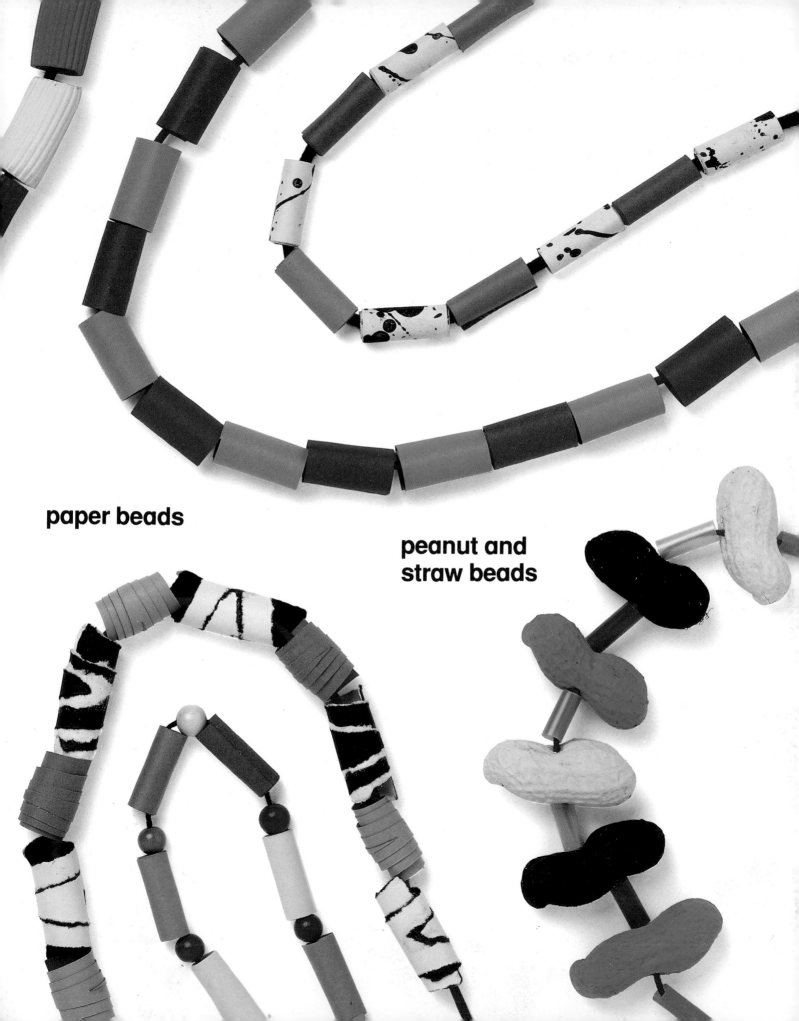

paper beads

peanut and straw beads

10 Cake

Here's a delicious way to play with patterns! Ask a grown-up to help you cover the top of a cake with soft icing. Use a collection of sweets to decorate the top.

Shapes and Colours

First decide which sweets you are going to use. Which ones look good together? Which are your favourites?

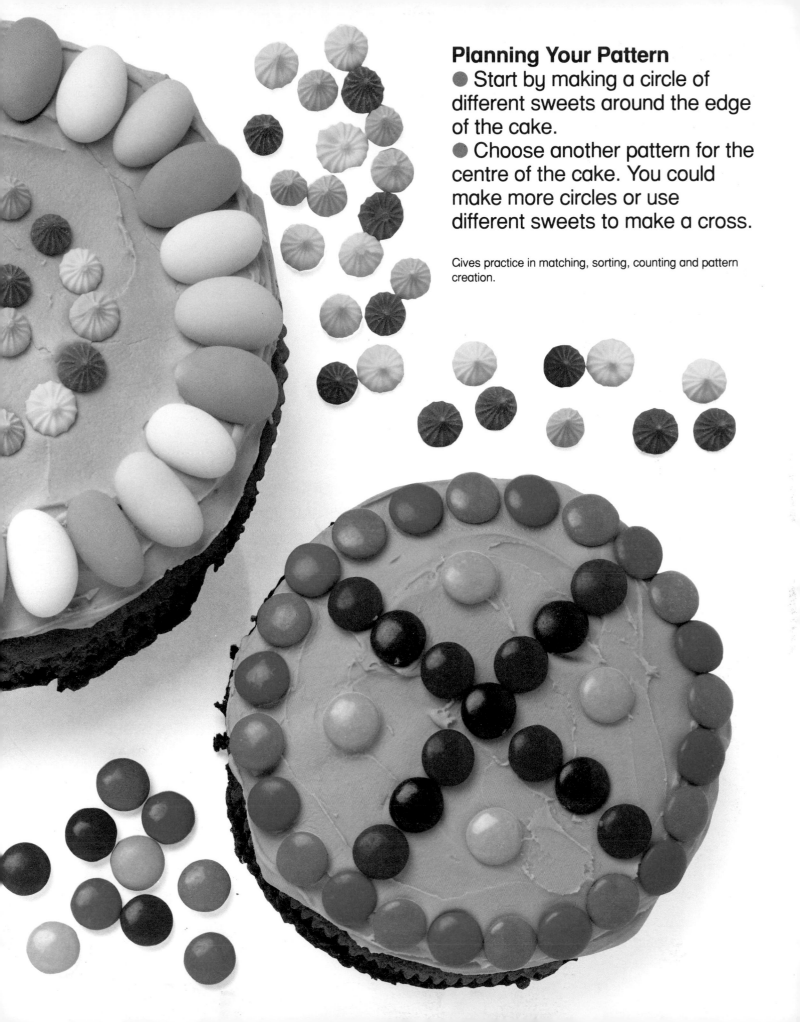

Planning Your Pattern

● Start by making a circle of different sweets around the edge of the cake.

● Choose another pattern for the centre of the cake. You could make more circles or use different sweets to make a cross.

Gives practice in matching, sorting, counting and pattern creation.

12 Weaving

Some of the clothes you wear are made from woven fabrics. These fabrics are made on large machines called looms. You can do your own weaving at home using a simple cardboard loom. Use brightly coloured wool or strips of felt. Can you see the pattern the threads make?

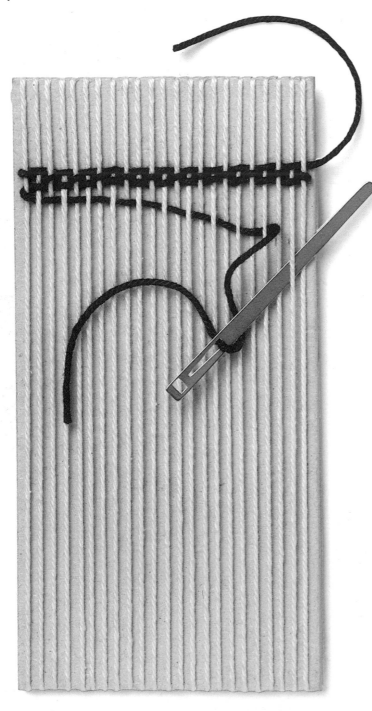

Loom
● Ask a grown-up to cut a piece of card and make notches in both ends.
● Wind a length of wool around the card. The notches will keep it in place. Tie the ends of the wool at the back.

Over and Under
● Ask a grown-up to thread a large, blunt needle with a length of wool.
● Weave the needle under the first thread, over the second and so on until you reach the other side.
● Bring the needle back the other way. Weave it under the threads you went over before, and over those you went under. Push the rows together.
● When you have finished, cut the threads at the back to take your weaving off. Tie the ends together to stop the weaving from coming apart.

Gives practice in creating patterns.

You can make a pattern with woven paper too! Find some fairly stiff coloured paper to weave with.

Simple Pattern

● Fold a piece of paper in half.
● Make a row of cuts along the folded edge. Unfold the paper.
● Cut some strips of another colour. Weave these strips over and under the slits you have made.

Diagonal Stripes

● Take another piece of paper and make diagonal cuts. Weave strips through the slits. Does the pattern look the same?
● You could use a piece of paper weaving to make a card for a friend.

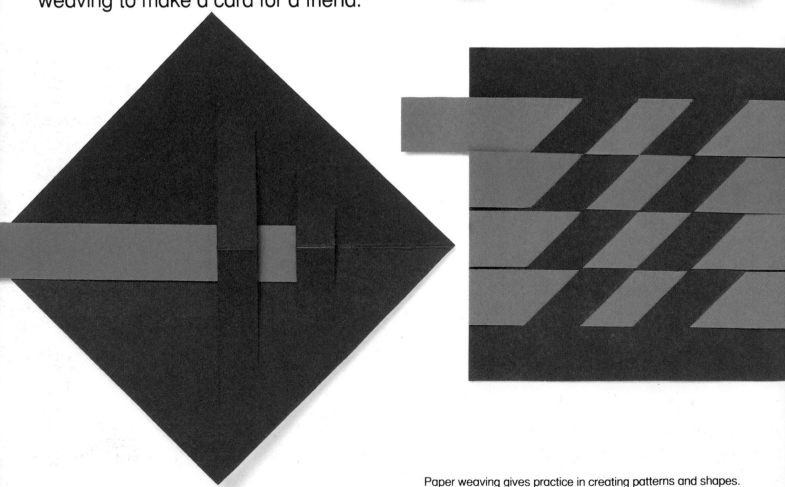

Paper weaving gives practice in creating patterns and shapes.

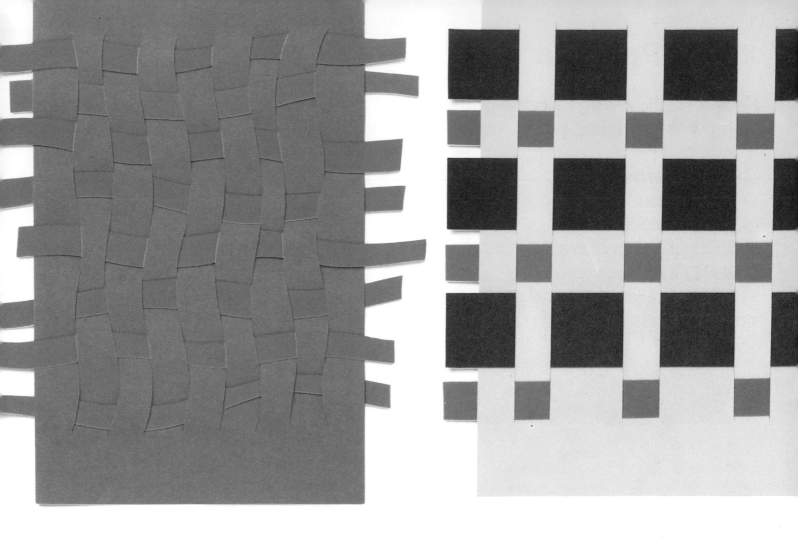

Wavy Stripes

Ask a grown-up to cut wavy slits in a piece of paper. You will also need some wavy strips in a different colour. Weave the strips as before.

Tartan Stripes

Cut two slits close together in a piece of folded paper. Leave a gap, then cut two more slits close together and so on. Weave thick and thin strips of coloured paper in and out of the slits.

Zig-zag Stripes

Ask a grown-up to make zig-zag slits in the paper with a craft knife. Weave straight strips through the slits.

16 Dot Patterns

Here's another way to make patterns using wool, glue and pins.

Glue Patterns

● Make a pattern with a few dots of glue on a piece of card.
● Take a length of wool. Press one end into the glue.
● Guide the wool around the glue pattern, pressing it down as you go.

● How many different sorts of patterns can you make?

Pin Patterns

● Ask a grown-up to arrange a pattern of pins on a piece of strong card.

● Take a length of wool and tie it carefully to one of the outside pins.

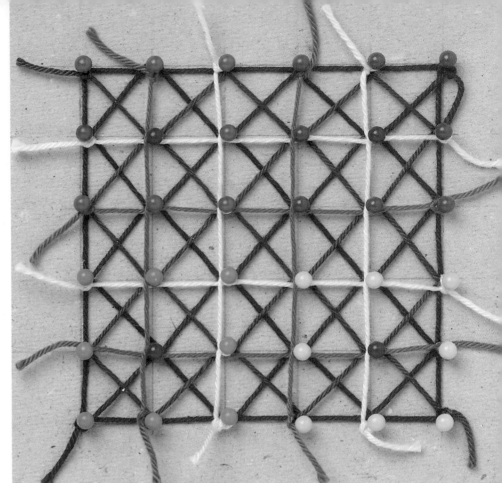

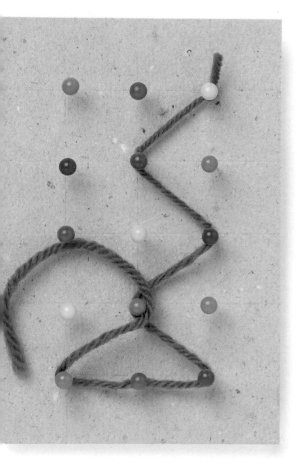

● Stretch the wool around the pins, twisting it on the pins to keep it in position. When you reach the edge, tie the end of the wool and cut off any extra.

● Try using different colours of wool to make pin patterns.

Gives practice in creating patterns and shapes.

Paper Cuts

You can make some amazing patterns by folding and cutting paper.

Fold and Cut
● Fold a piece of paper in half and then in half again. Cut a small piece out of one edge. Unfold the paper.

● To make a more complicated pattern, make several cuts along the edges before unfolding the paper.

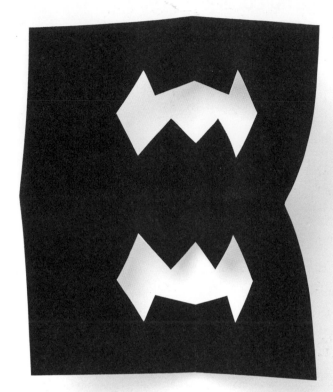

Concertina Folds

● Cut a long strip of paper.
Make some small folds backwards
and forwards. The strip will open out
like a concertina.

● Make cuts in the folded paper.
Be careful not to cut off too much from
the folded edge.

● Open the paper out.

● Now try making a more complicated
pattern, like this row of people.

Gives practice in creating patterns. Introduces the idea of reflective
symmetry.

20 Tiles

Each of these tiles has a very simple design, but you can arrange them to make all sorts of patterns.

Designing the Tiles
● Ask a grown up to cut out some squares of card all the same size.
● Choose a simple design and paint each square exactly the same.

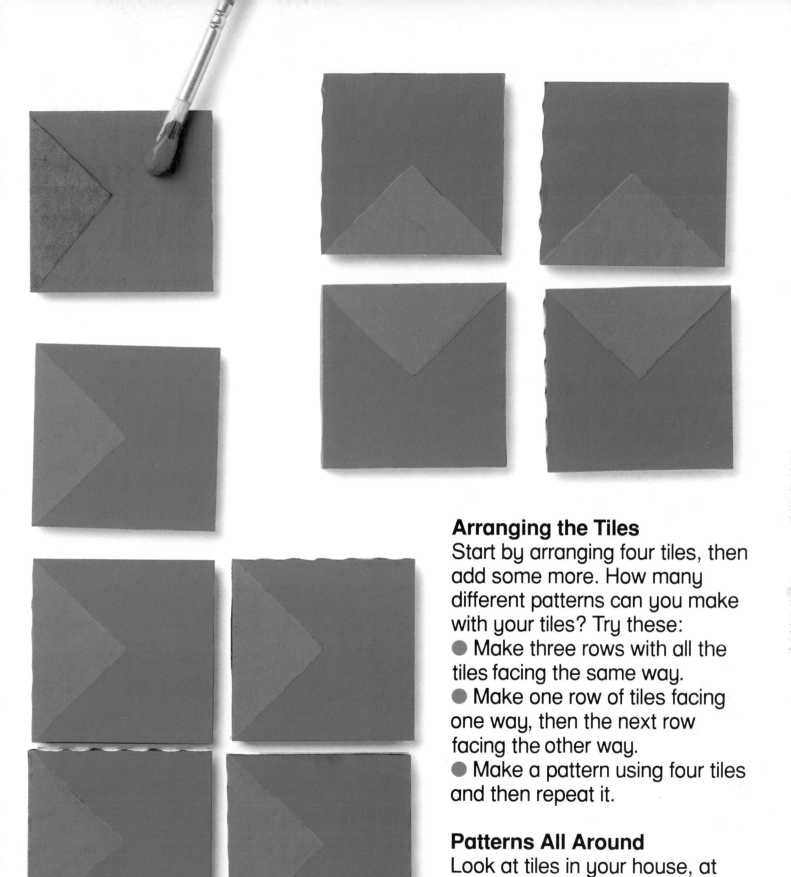

Arranging the Tiles

Start by arranging four tiles, then add some more. How many different patterns can you make with your tiles? Try these:
● Make three rows with all the tiles facing the same way.
● Make one row of tiles facing one way, then the next row facing the other way.
● Make a pattern using four tiles and then repeat it.

Patterns All Around

Look at tiles in your house, at school and when you are outside. Do they make a pattern?

Gives practice in creating patterns and shapes.

22 Mosaics

These coloured shapes fit together to make patterns.

Making the Shapes
Ask a grown-up to cut some shapes from coloured paper or thin card. They could draw around the shapes shown on this page.

Fitting Together
● Sort the shapes out. Put all the triangles together, all the diamonds, and so on.

● See how shapes that are the same fit together. Use different colours to make a pattern.

● Now try fitting two different shapes together. Which shapes fit well?

● Try fitting all the different shapes together. How many patterns can you make?

Gives practice in creating patterns. Introduces the idea that some shapes tessellate, or fit together without any gaps.

24 Repeating Patterns

Make a sheet of wrapping paper by decorating it with a pattern. Pick a shape and repeat it lots of times.

String Blocks
Glue a long length of string on to a piece of card to make a print block. Cover the block with thick paint and press it on to a sheet of paper.

Potato Prints
Think of a simple shape and draw it on a piece of paper. Ask a grown-up to slice a potato in half and cut the shape from one half, so that it sticks up from the potato. Use a paintbrush to cover the shape with thick paint. Press the potato on to a sheet of paper. Lift the potato off and put some more paint on. Print the shape lots of times.

Stencils

Ask a grown-up to cut a stencil like our tulip out of strong card. Place the stencil on a sheet of paper. Hold it down carefully with one hand, or tape it in place. Dab paint over the stencil. Remove the stencil carefully and repeat until you have a pattern.

Gives practice in creating repeat patterns.

26 Mirror Prints

Simple Prints
● Fold a piece of paper in half.
● Open the paper out and put a blob of paint on one side of the fold.
● Fold the paper along the fold line and press down firmly.
● Open the paper out.

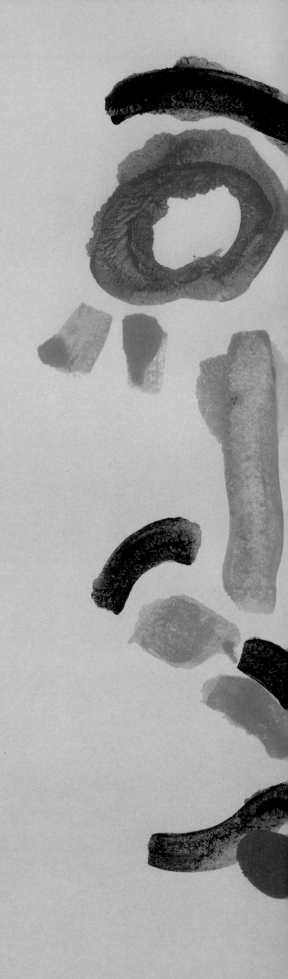

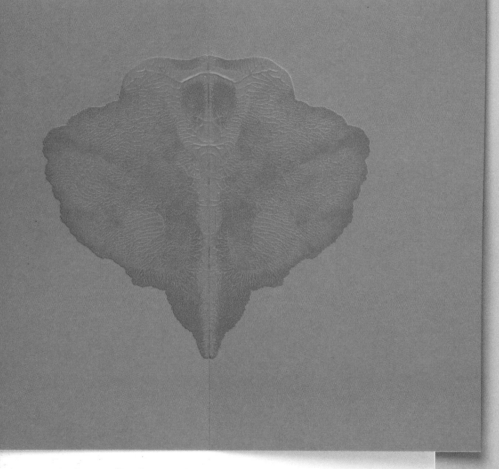

Mixing Colours
● Try making some prints using different colours.
● Use one colour at a time, and allow the paint to dry before adding another colour.

Gives practice in matching, and left and right. Introduces reflective symmetry.

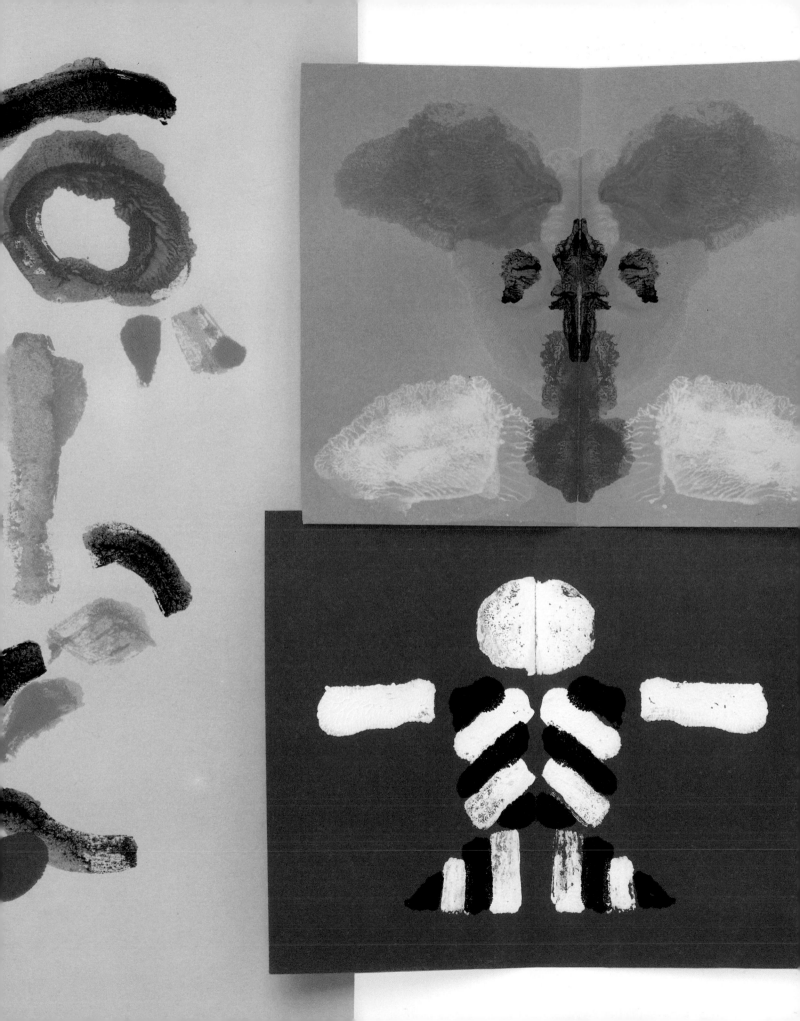

Ask a grown-up to cut a simple shape from half a potato. Cover the shape with fabric paint. Carefully press it down on to a plain T-shirt or sock. Repeat to make a printed pattern.

Try printing with a different shape using another colour. You can vary your pattern by printing shapes in different directions.

Read the instructions on the fabric paint before you start printing. When the paint is dry, ask a grown-up to iron your T-shirt on the wrong side. You will then be able to wash it without the paint coming off.

Gives practice in creating repeat patterns.

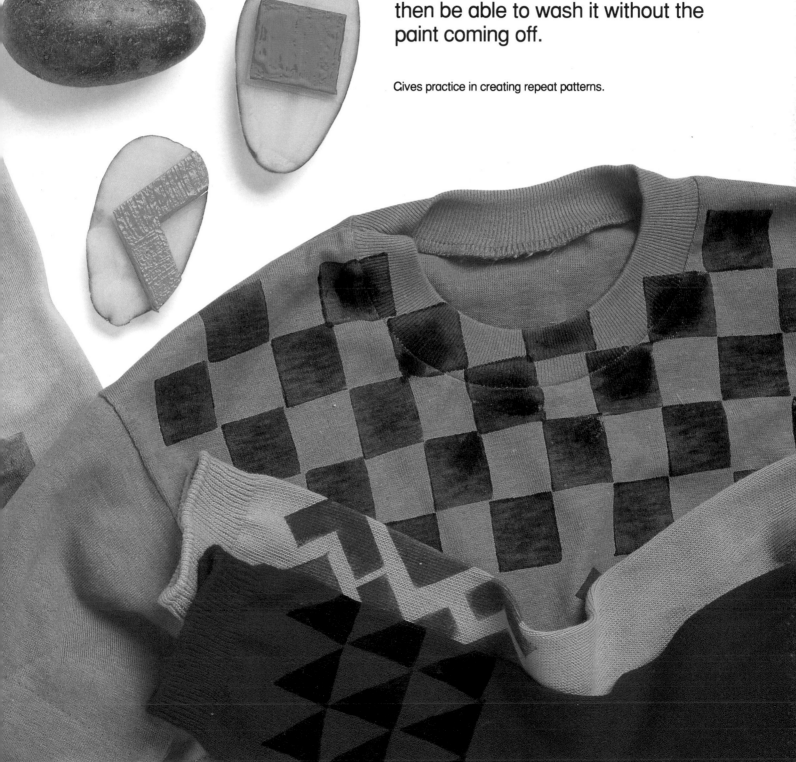

30 Stationery

Try using different types of patterns to decorate cards, writing paper and envelopes. Use brightly coloured paper, and make sure you leave enough room to write on! You could use some of the patterns you have found in this book, or make up some new ones.

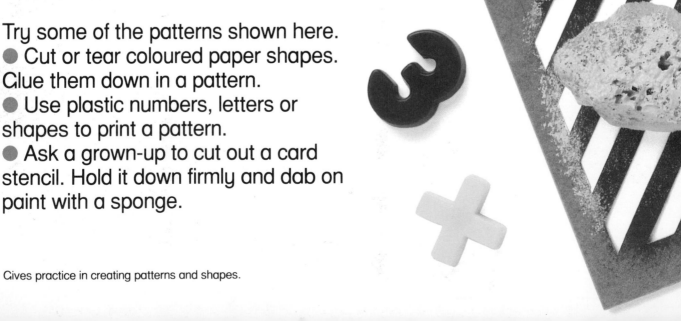

Try some of the patterns shown here.
● Cut or tear coloured paper shapes. Glue them down in a pattern.
● Use plastic numbers, letters or shapes to print a pattern.
● Ask a grown-up to cut out a card stencil. Hold it down firmly and dab on paint with a sponge.

Gives practice in creating patterns and shapes.

Index

Editor: Diane James
Photography: Toby
Text: Claire Watts

First published in Great Britain in 1992 by
Two-Can Publishing Ltd
346 Old Street
London EC1V 9NQ
in association with Scholastic Publications Ltd

Pbk ISBN 1-85434-177-4
Hbk ISBN 1-85434-192-8

Patterns and the National Curriculum

Creating the patterns shown in this book is directly helpful to National Curriculum mathematics. Doing these activities involves interpreting and carrying out instructions, appraising work, and developing confidence in craft skills. Thus children's involvement in other National Curriculum subjects, such as science, technology and art can be supported by having fun with this book.

Contents

Consultants

Wendy and David Clemson are experienced teachers and researchers. They have written many successful books on mathematics and are regular contributors to "eC", the educational supplement of "The Guardian" newspaper. Wendy is currently pursuing her interests in the primary curriculum and is working on a variety of writing projects for children, parents and teachers, with a particular emphasis on the early years. David is Reader in Primary Education at Liverpool John Moores University.